dinosaurs

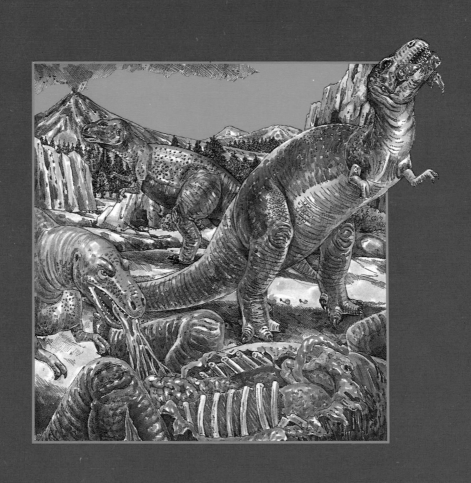

SERIES EDITOR	DAVID SALARIYA
BOOK EDITOR	APRIL McCROSKIE
CONSULTANT	JOHN COOPER

W FRANKLIN WATTS

First published in 1995
by Franklin Watts
a division of the Watts Publishing Group Ltd
96 Leonard Street
London EC2A 4XD

This edition published 2001

ISBN 0 7496 4265 3
Dewey Classification 567.9

© THE SALARIYA BOOK COMPANY LTD MCMXCV

Printed in Belgium

A CIP catalogue record for this book is available from the British Library.

dinosaurs

Written by
SCOTT STEEDMAN
Illustrated by
CAROLYN SCRACE

Series Created & Designed by
DAVID SALARIYA

WATTS BOOKS
London • Sydney

CONTENTS

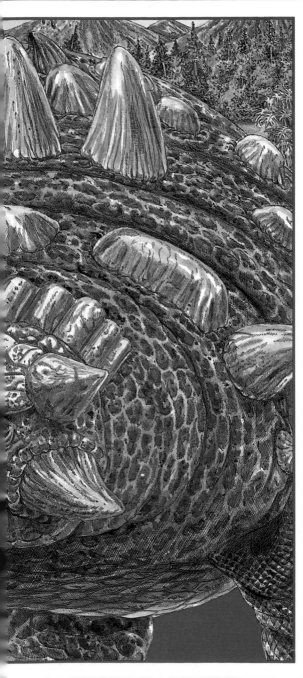

The Dinosaur Age

(the Mesozoic era) began 225 million years ago. At that time Earth was covered in thick forests, dusty plains and shallow seas. The climate was much hotter than it is now. There were no mammals, flowering plants, or birds.

Among the shrubs and trees, the first dinosaurs searched for food. The dinosaurs were reptiles and so are close relatives of today's snakes and crocodiles with their scaly skin. Dinosaurs would survive on Earth for the next 160 million years.

People who study life-forms from the past are called palaeontologists.

This worker is using a brush to clear away tiny fragments from a bone.

The bare bones are usually all that is left of a dinosaur. All the soft parts like the skin and organs have rotted away. Only the hardest bits of bones, teeth and claws are turned to stone, or fossilized. Experts dig up these fragments in search of clues to help them put the beast together again. The size of one bone can tell us how big the dinosaur was. Ridges and grooves show how the muscles and blood vessels fitted together. One tooth may be enough to show what the animal ate. This giant jigsaw puzzle can take years to complete.

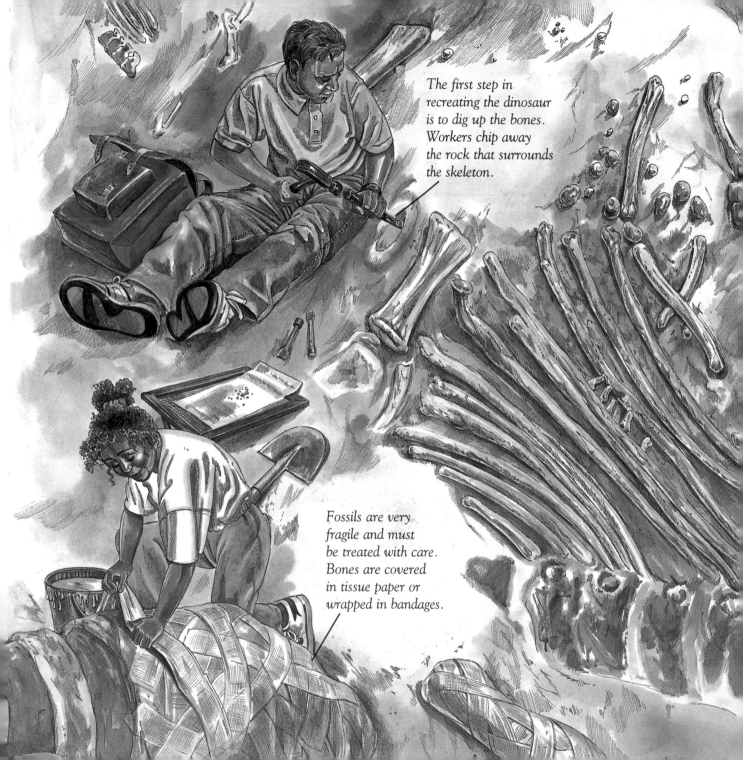

The first step in recreating the dinosaur is to dig up the bones. Workers chip away the rock that surrounds the skeleton.

Fossils are very fragile and must be treated with care. Bones are covered in tissue paper or wrapped in bandages.

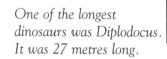

One of the longest dinosaurs was Diplodocus. It was 27 metres long.

The Mesozoic Era was divided into 3 periods – Triassic, Jurassic and Cretaceous.

Triassic period
245-208 million years ago

Jurassic period
208-146 million years ago

Cretaceous period
146-65 million years ago

Dinosaurs are the largest animals to have walked on Earth. The biggest ones weighed ten times more than the heaviest elephant. The smallest dinosaurs were no bigger than chickens. There were hundreds of different dinosaurs but not all of them lived at the same time.

The first dinosaurs appeared in the Triassic period, from 245 to 208 million years ago. The climate was dry and warm.

Some of the smallest and largest species appeared in the Jurassic period, from 208 to 146 million years ago. Earth was more lush.

A huge variety of dinosaurs existed in the Cretaceous period, from 146 to 65 million years ago.

Pteranodon – a
flying reptile.

Some experts believe
birds – and not
reptiles – are the
dinosaurs' closest
living relatives.
The Archaeopteryx
had reptile features
but it had feathers
like a modern bird.

Modern pigeon

Some dinosaurs
were meat eaters
(carnivores), others
were plant eaters
(herbivores).

Deinonychus was a
fast-moving hunter.

Stegosaurus

Modern
crocodile

If we compare a
modern crocodile to a
Stegosaurus we see some
similarities. But the crocodile
is smaller with legs that stick
out sideways from
its body.

11

Carnivorous giants hunted

other dinosaurs – even if they were plant eaters much bigger than they were themselves. They would follow a herd of grazing herbivores, and then wait for a small or weak member of the pack to wander off on its own. The meat eaters then moved in for the kill.

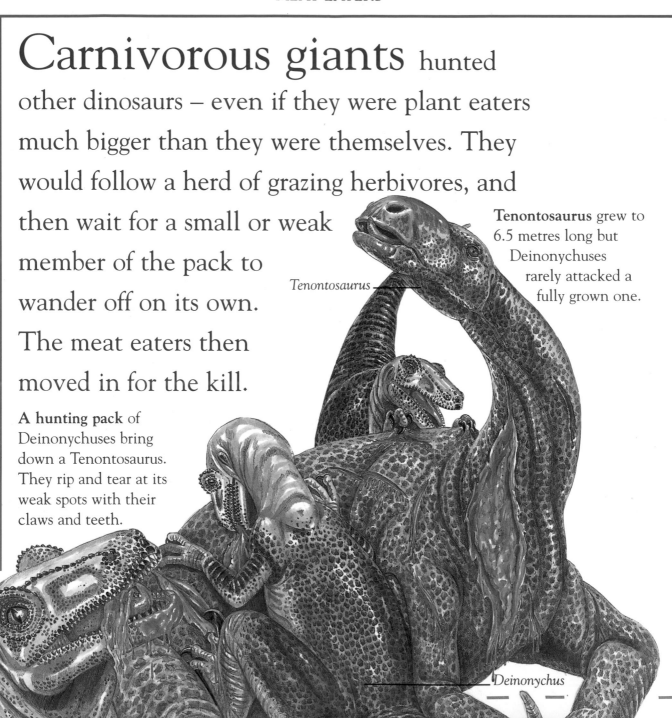

Tenontosaurus

Tenontosaurus grew to 6.5 metres long but Deinonychuses rarely attacked a fully grown one.

A hunting pack of Deinonychuses bring down a Tenontosaurus. They rip and tear at its weak spots with their claws and teeth.

Deinonychus

The hunter had to move fast – the rotting flesh was very smelly and brought other dinosaurs running for their share.

Daspletosaurus was a smaller relative of Tyrannosaurus, reaching 9 metres in length. It lived 75 to 65 million years ago in the Cretaceous period.

Albertosaurus also lived in the Cretaceous period and looked similar to Daspletosaurus. It hunted dinosaurs such as the Triceratops.

Tyrannosaurus rex lived in the Cretaceous period, from 146 to 65 million years ago.

Tyrannosaurus rex probably hunted alone. But it may also have been a scavenger, joining other dinosaurs to finish off their kills.

Daspletosaurus

Tyrannosaurus rex

Albertosaurus

Tyrannosaurus attacks

Triceratops uses horns for defence.

Struthiomimus chases insects.

Pachycephalosaurus males butt heads.

Resting on stomach   *Starting to rise*   *Throwing head back*   *Fully upright*

Massive jaws and teeth helped Tyrannosaurus to rip great chunks of flesh out of its prey. It did not chew its food, but swallowed it whole.

Tyrannosaurus sprinted after its prey on powerful back legs. The tail helped balance the weight of its massive head.

Tyrannosaurus rex was the biggest meat eater ever to walk on Earth. Its name means "king tyrant lizard". It grew 14 metres long and 5 metres tall. It hunted other dinosaurs, probably by hiding and then pouncing on them. It had a mouth full of nasty teeth and strong back legs with sharp claws.

Tyrannosaurus runs after a Parasaurolophus.

On pages 16 and 17, a Compsognathus chases its prey.

15

Long
neck

The heavy tail could
be lifted off the ground.

Plateosaurus ate pebbles which
helped grind up food in its stomach.

Living in a herd would
have helped protect the
Plateosaurus against
attacks from predators.

The biggest dinosaurs were the

vegetarians. A slow-moving creature like Plateosaurus
had to eat a lot of plants every day just to survive. To
digest all this, it needed an enormous stomach and
intestines. But Plateosaurus was small compared to the
real giants such as Brachiosaurus. This species weighed
80 tonnes and its neck was 9 metres long.

Cheek pouch

Small head

A Plateosaurus could walk on all four legs or by standing up on its strong back legs. Standing upright it could stretch its neck to feed on high leaves that other dinosaurs could not reach.

The thumb ended in a broad, powerful claw. Plateosaurus must have used this to fight off meat eating dinosaurs.

Thumb claw

Diamond-shaped
plates

To protect its
rear, Stegosaurus
swished its tail
spikes from
side to side.

Strong pillar-
like legs

Small, low-
slung head

The plates were not used for
defence. They had holes like a
sponge and were probably rich
in blood vessels. Some experts
think that Stegosaurus used its
plates like a radiator to heat up
or cool down its body.

Stegosaurus means
'roof lizard' because
people used to think
that the plates on its
back overlapped like
roof tiles.

A small brain meant that
Stegosaurus moved slowly
and that its senses and reflexes
were poor. But this was not a
great problem and they were
common for nearly 70
million years.

Tail spikes

Stegosaurus remains were found only in western North America, in what is now Colorado, Utah and Wyoming. It lived about 150 million years ago in the late Jurassic period.

A Stegosaurus had a big body but a small brain. This lumbering dinosaur was 7 metres long and weighed 1.5 tonnes, but its brain was the size of a walnut. A crest of jagged plates ran in a staggered line down its back. It also had long spikes on its tail which it could swing around like a club.

Stegosaurus fed on ferns, cycads and other low-level vegetation. It had small teeth and weak jaw muscles so it did not chew much. Instead, it had a huge stomach where food was left to ferment for several days.

Wide neck frill

Tongue

Powerful jaw

Five toes on
front feet

Shorter
front
legs

Many dinosaurs laid eggs –
just like modern reptiles and birds.
This fact was proved in the 1920s, when
the nests of a colony of Protoceratops were
found in the Gobi Desert in Mongolia.
The female laid eggs in a hollow scooped out
in the sand. She then sat on them to keep them
warm. Turn the page to see a nest and hatchlings.

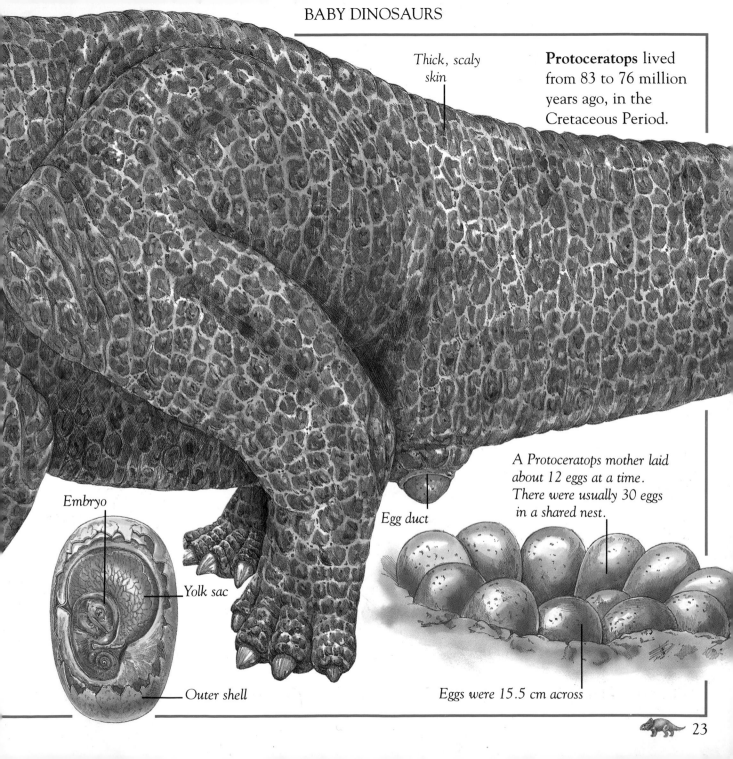

Thick, scaly skin

Protoceratops lived from 83 to 76 million years ago, in the Cretaceous Period.

Embryo

Yolk sac

Outer shell

Egg duct

A Protoceratops mother laid about 12 eggs at a time. There were usually 30 eggs in a shared nest.

Eggs were 15.5 cm across

Maiasaura mothers had to be on the lookout for hungry dinosaurs who would eat their young. The mothers may even have shared babysitting duties.

Maiasauras roamed the high plains of North America. Fossils suggest that tens of thousands of animals may have gathered together for safety in numbers.

Horny crest above the eyes

Maiasaura was a duck-billed dinosaur that could walk upright.

It is likely that the fat end of the eggs, where the baby hatched, faced out of the nest. This way the baby Maiasaura could get out more easily.

Babies were born with small teeth and were able to eat solid food straight away.

Like many modern mammals, baby Maiasauras had large eyes.

The Maiasaura nests were close together. The average distance between them was 7 metres – the length of a fully grown Maiasaura mother.

Fossilized nests and babies are very rare. This is probably because most dinosaurs built their nests in hard-to-reach places. The Maiasaura nests were discovered in 1978.

Mothers brought food for their young before they went out to forage for their own.

Finally the eggs hatched and tiny, perfectly formed dinosaur babies came crawling out. The drawings on these pages show a nest of Maiasaura dinosaurs in Montana, USA. This is how it may have looked 80-75 million years ago (Cretaceous period). Some of these babies would have been in the nest for weeks. Their parents brought them food, and sat on them to keep them warm.

Maiasaura means 'good mother lizard'. Dinosaur babies were not very big but they grew quickly. When they left the nest, the babies may have walked in the centre of the herd, so that they were protected by a ring of fully grown dinosaurs.

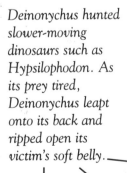

Deinonychus had a large head full of big jagged teeth. Its front legs ended in sharp, slender claws.

Horny beaks and sharp claws helped many dinosaurs to bite off vegetation or catch their prey. Plant eaters such as Triceratops and Psittacosaurus had toothless beaks to help them crunch through even the toughest tree trunks.

Psittacosaurus ——

Deinonychus hunted slower-moving dinosaurs such as Hypsilophodon. As its prey tired, Deinonychus leapt onto its back and ripped open its victim's soft belly.

Psittacosaurus means 'parrot lizard'. This plant eater lived from 98 to 90 million years ago. It had a strong skull, a beak and muscular jaws for chewing its food.

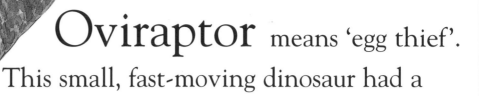

Oviraptor means 'egg thief'.

This small, fast-moving dinosaur had a horny beak and long, curving claws. They may have used these to crack open the eggs of other dinosaurs.

Oviraptor got its name because experts have always believed that this dinosaur ate the eggs of other dinosaurs.

There is no evidence that Oviraptor ate eggs of its own kind. Other dinosaurs such as Coleophysis ate their own babies.

Three-fingered hand

Broken dinosaur egg

Bony crest

Sharp prong

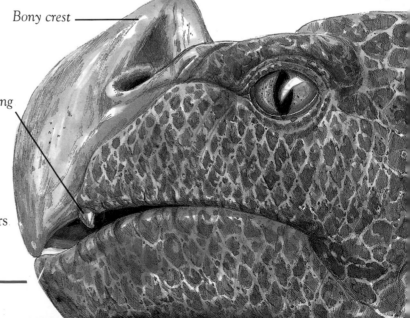

Experts recently discovered a fossilized Oviraptor egg. It was found near a place where an adult Oviraptor skeleton was found in 1923. Perhaps this means that Oviraptors were not egg thieves but simply looked after their own babies.

Euoplocephalus had a big, strong tail club that it used as a weapon in self-defence. If a meat-eating Albertosaurus kept attacking it, Euoplocephalus would swing its heavy tail at the attacker's legs. The Albertosaurus would be knocked to the ground. Crippled and helpless it would be eaten by other carnivorous dinosaurs.

The tail club was solid bone and was very heavy. The rest of the tail was relatively light, so the dinosaur could swing it freely.

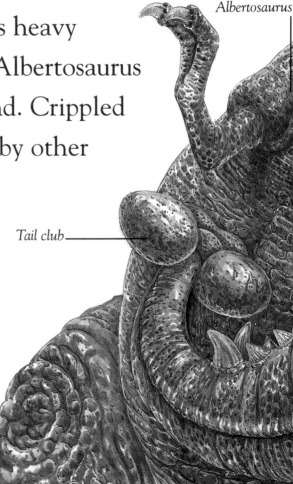

Albertosaurus

Tail club

Kentrosaurus

Kentrosaurus was a small dinosaur covered in long spines. It would back into its attackers to defend itself.

One of the best ways to avoid being eaten was to run away! Lesothosaurus was small and moved very quickly.

To protect their babies, a herd of Chasmosauruses would form a circle. Predators would see just horns and armoured plates.

Euoplocephalus

Euoplocephalus was armoured heavily. Its head was covered in spikes, and spines and bony plates pricked out of its back and tail.

Triceratops lived in North America 70 million years ago. It lived at the same time as giant predators such as Tyrannosaurus. It grew to 9 metres long and weighed 5.4 tonnes.

With its massive horns, Styracosaurus was one of the strangest looking dinosaurs.

Open woodland

Thick, scaly skin

Horns could reach 1.5 metres long.

Single nose horn

Heavy tail

Stubby legs

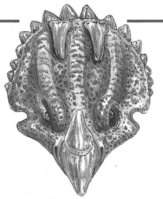

Centrosaurus

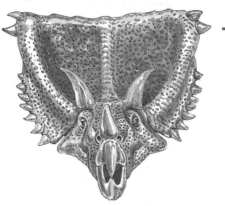

Chasmosaurus

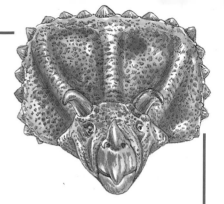

Anchiceratops

Centrosaurus was another ceratopsid dinosaur. This meant that it had a collection of horns and spikes.

The huge neck frill protected the animal's back as well as anchoring its strong jaw muscles. This is Chasmosaurus.

Anchiceratops had three large horns. It was a close relative of Triceratops. It moved slowly around the woodlands of western North America.

Triceratops had a huge head

armed with three sharp horns – one above each eye and a third on the tip of its nose. It also had a neck frill lined with bony spikes. These spikes were purely for protection. Triceratops and its many relatives were slow-moving vegetarians who did not attack other dinosaurs for food. They used their large horny beaks to snip off plant stems and shoots.

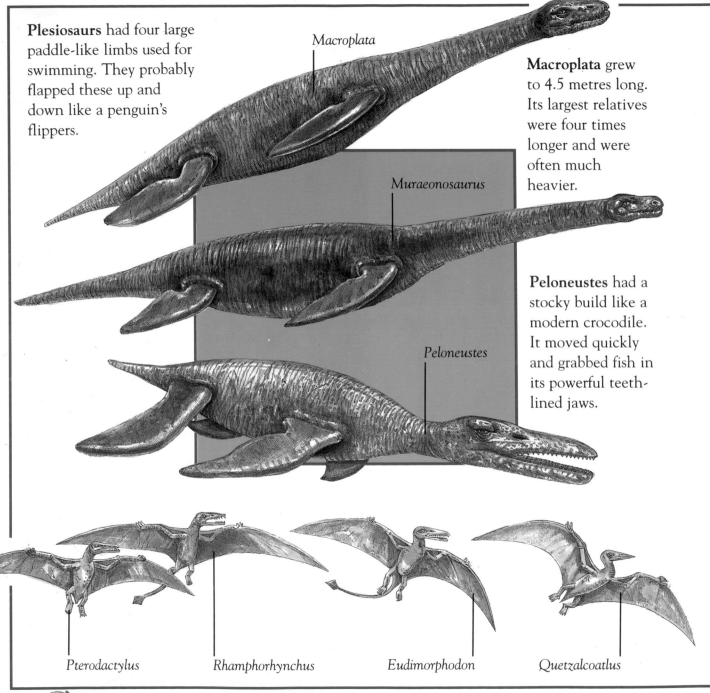

Plesiosaurs had four large paddle-like limbs used for swimming. They probably flapped these up and down like a penguin's flippers.

Macroplata

Macroplata grew to 4.5 metres long. Its largest relatives were four times longer and were often much heavier.

Muraeonosaurus

Peloneustes had a stocky build like a modern crocodile. It moved quickly and grabbed fish in its powerful teeth-lined jaws.

Peloneustes

Pterodactylus

Rhamphorhynchus

Eudimorphodon

Quetzalcoatlus

In prehistoric times, flying and swimming reptiles filled the seas and skies. Though they were not dinosaurs, they were related to these land-bound giants.

The pterosaurs were the only reptiles that could fly. Sea reptiles included massive turtles, ichthyosaurs (fish reptiles) and long-necked monsters called plesiosaurs (ribbon reptiles).

Elasmosaurus was 13 metres long. Over half of this was its snake-like neck. It had a pointed tail, not a flat one like a whale has today.

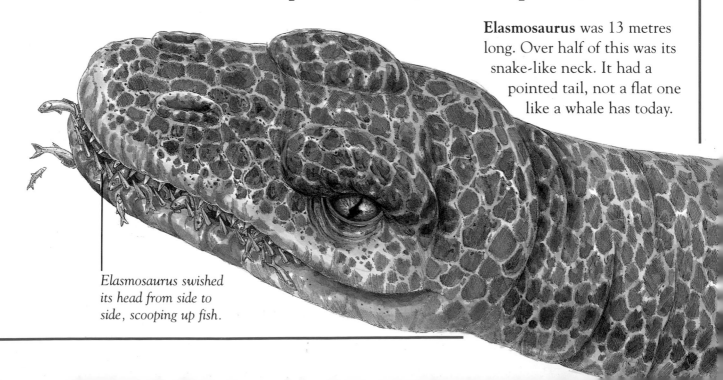

Elasmosaurus swished its head from side to side, scooping up fish.

The meteor was about 15 km across. Most of it probably broke up in space but as it reached Earth there was a huge explosion. This created a huge cloud of dust and water vapour.

The dust cloud spread across the globe and skies turned blood red. After that total darkness descended.

The darkness lasted for many months. The cloud may have held poisonous gases and most plants died.

Plant eaters starved slowly. The largest ones, the dinosaurs, died first – smaller ones lived longer.

About 64 million years ago,

the dinosaurs, along with most flying and swimming reptiles, disappeared forever. What disaster killed them so suddenly? Many scientists believe that a giant meteor – a chunk of rock from space – hit the Earth. The skies were clogged with dust that blocked the sun and caused a darkness that may have lasted many months – maybe even years. Animals like the dinosaurs were wiped out completely.

Meat eaters ate the dead plant eaters. But these were all eaten quickly so the meat eaters starved too.

After months, or even years, the vapour cloud lifted. Insects, small reptiles and mammals were the only survivors.

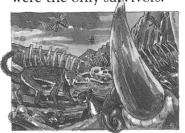

Millions of years later, mammals and birds have developed into an incredible variety of new species.

USEFUL WORDS

Carnivore An animal that eats meat.

Cretaceous The period from 146 to 65 million years ago. Dinosaurs disappeared at the end of this period.

Cycad A palm-like plant found in tropical areas.

Fossil The preserved remains of an animal or plant that lived millions of years ago.

Hatchling A newly hatched baby animal.

Herbivore An animal that eats plants.

Ichthyosaurs Prehistoric swimming reptiles that resembled dolphins.

Jurassic The period from 208 to 146 million years ago. The biggest dinosaurs lived at this time, and the first birds developed.

Mammal A warm-blooded animal.

Mesozoic era The age of dinosaurs, from 245 to 65 million years ago.

Mongolia A large country in eastern Asia between China and Russia.

Plesiosaurs Prehistoric

swimming reptiles with long, slender bodies.

Predator An animal that hunts and preys on other animals.

Prehistoric Existing before written history began.

Prey An animal that is eaten by a predator.

Pterosaurs Prehistoric flying reptiles closely related to dinosaurs.

Triassic The period from 245 to 208 million years ago. The first dinosaurs appeared.

INDEX